MW00941445

RIOTING
AT DAWN

RIOTING
AT DAWN

ROYCE HALL

Copyright © 2015 Royce Hall
ISBN- 13: 978-1512347852
All Rights Reserved

No part of this book may be reproduced, stored in a retrieval
system or transmitted by any means without written permission
of the author.

First published by Royce Hall
Back cover photo by Chad Finley of Finley Photos

In celebration of this being my first collection of poetry, this book is dedicated to my mother, Dr. Vivian H. Royster for every ounce of love, encouragement and effortless support, you continue to shower me with day after day, Melanie for encouraging the process, May Reign for every bit of guidance throughout building my body of art. To every sister and brother of Black Gold, I dedicate this book to you, to us.

This body of work is in memory of my son Joshua Kalonji-Alimayu Royster, my grandparents Henry and Emma Lou Hall, and my uncle Eddie L. Hall.

Contents

4/9/14

For The Men of Vineyards

Somewhere, someone binds
Squeezing life
Between fabric and ace bandages
Risking possible long-term damages
Numbing the unwanted
All for the sensation of being
Getting as close to living
As they can
Flattening what may stand
Smoothing edges and squaring curves
Tightening torsos
Shortening breaths
Limiting respiration
Decreasing circulation
The death and rebirth discovered in transitioning
Coping, temporary satisfaction is prescribed
Vital organs deprived
At the desire to...feel...alive
Contorting to erase what may be seen
Tampering with the rhythm of the heart in me
To design and align the heart of me
The throbbing of inflaming kidneys
Liver and spleen
Somewhere we bind
Dying to pass
Until we are able
To remove that which may confine
Us to our past
Someone, somewhere binds

Until scalpels release existence
And recovery reveals our divine
Reminded that every grape
Was stomped after being pulled from the vine
To create the sweetest of wine.

4/10/14

Resting Places & Trash Day

Today, I cleaned
Ridding my environment of dust
Dirt
Grime
The unnecessary
And you
Laundered sheets
Opened windows
On hands and knees
Scrubbing away smudges
Smears and pain
Dried puddles and water stains
From tears
From years
Of my allowing you
To create clutter
And unload your baggage in my space
While I created for you
A place
Of safety
Today, I cleaned
Let Sade sing
And crowned myself king
Of sorrow...

4/11/14

Full Bottle, Empty Heart

...we made promises to always embrace
That Burberry Touch perfume
I bought for you is still in my closet
You never got it
And strangely enough
Just as the name of the fragrance suggests
It's something we no longer do...

4/10/14

Mother's Growing Babies

Life's journey moves so fast
Shout out to those enduring motion sickness
Mad respect to the caterpillar for knowing when to hibernate
And the butterfly for knowing when to break the seal on its
     cocoon
Mother nature surrounds us with messengers
Don't miss her delivery while
Expecting a certain type of package
There's a fine line between tearing away the wrapper and
     unraveling at the seams
Know when to retreat
Know when to spread your wings
Prepare to endure earthquakes and turbulence
It's imperative that we go through and get through
The metamorphosis.

4/12/14

Charles Ellis

I was born when winter came
He never did
Tried to be him
Beat him
But I could never be as bitterly cold
as his December winds
Left his nest egg
Resting on the branch's edge
For snow storms to taunt
During its hatching
Summer came
Autumn came
Spring even
But every winter
The chills aggravate the splinter in my shell
A reminder as tart as his absence
I wait for newness to fill the air
Like the egg nesting
Resting
Still on the edge
Waiting to be rescued
By father time...
By...by...dad.

4/15/14

Trap Music

We survive between beats and breaks
The rhythm of struggle and up rise
White sheets and hoods disguised as heroes in capes
And when the records skip
We switch to tapes
And boogie to the cacophony
Found in replays and outtakes
Turning the other cheek
B sides and blanks
When the frame is broken
Taught to bandage the case
From Till to Martin
And when we're done marchin'
How many does it take to be discovered in alleys or in the belly of
    marshlands
For us to compose our own measure
Take back our own treasure
This earth we've given birth to
Loss to conductors with knight sticks
Burning crosses
In places we should be able to stand ground
But if the turn tables aren't shook
Or bumped into
Who's maintaining the crescendo of our sound...

4/8/14

Living Water

Rainy nights
Easy conversation
Kindred star people
Reflecting black sunshine
Discovering that there's more to life.
And, this downpour during Atlanta nights
Is simply timeless
We live in the light
No matter where darkness is
Every word exchanged is photosynthesis
On fertile ground
We plant seeds
And harvest with ease
Even when seasons change and we let the wind blow
Know
Our crop will keep us abundantly fed...

4/19/14

Scandal: For Sale

We
Darker than blue
Surviving the extensive pressing of coal
The reverse
The dress rehearsal
The brutal
The bruised
Ribs and flesh infused
The divided
The Middle Passage
We
The confiscated
The incarcerated
The shackled
We
The testimonials
The biggest scandal
That Shonda partially, inadvertently exposes without a clue
Minus million dollar contracts
And the juicy allure of entertainment
Only wooden floors
Boards
Breeding beds
and a queen, a mother, a sister, a daughter
womanhood slaughtered
childhood taken
Invaded
Annihilated
episode after episode

400 years ago and counting
No set
No premiere
Only tears
Blood stained rags
Or affairs never mentioned
Families auctioned off and sold on store fronts
And we who watch
Guided by the guise
Of a love story brought to the forefront
From plantations to the oval office
The misery of such history
No dead presidents should ever allow it to make sense...

4/21/14

Beyond Spring

Show me your new
Untouched
Intimate
Close
Divine
Quiet for three seasons
Show me your warmth
Your awakening
Your light
After somnolence
Show me your free
Without anchor
Your release from hiding
Show me your flower
In full bloom
Your morning dew that glistens into June
Your sweetness
Nectar for sustaining
For tasting
Your petals that may brown in autumn
But rarely fall
And for you
I offer honey
Show me Oshun
Show me still waters
Running deep and strong
With sparkling
Inviting surfaces
Show me where your sun is

Show me why you precede summer
Your brave
Show me you'll stick around
Even during winters attempted chill
And the kill of green leaves
Show me you'll build
Shelter
Strong enough
To weather
The possibility
Of any
Change...

4/20/14

Sweet Reprise

Many of us feel as though we've experienced being broken in two
Then one day we breathe
and realize the pieces are still intact
and we survived
and it takes much courage to relinquish control
and be broken into
From heartbreaks to heartbeats
Surviving the rhythm to embrace the melody...

4/21/14

Submerge

And if your waters are currents I can swim in
Let me put more than my feet in
Find me in the deep end
And, on that, nothing depends...

4/22/14

In the Name of Love

Spare me of your rule books
Tires
Guidelines
Crystal balls
Extras
Past
What if's
Crosses through names
Deleted numbers
Those you've unfollowed
Plans b's
Horror stories
Why's
Lies
And who didn't's
The predictable
Spare me of safety zones
Flags
The obvious
Play outs
Fears
But not your militancy
To give the unknown
A chance...

4/23/14

K.I.T.

Honestly
I hate that your pic
Still sits
Next to your number
In my contacts list
And even more so
That I have yet
To muster up the strength
To erase it
But for some reason
A trace of you needs to remain
Close
An addiction
To which
I'm required a daily dose
Some sick
Twisted
Demented fix
Associated with
Each night cap
Text
Call
Emoji
Posing in my inbox
With this elixir
Magic potion
Causing commotion
Every time you reach out
I reply like, "Who is this?"

Fronting.
Knowing I could never forget you
And I know that smile
And those eyes
In that pic
Better than I know
My own
I just hate that
In your foolery
I thought I found solace
Thought I found home...

4/28/14

Bar One Aftermath

Confession
Silence
Seems
So
Visibly
Loud
Without
The
Sight
Of
Your
Smile
And
The
Sound
Of
Your
Laughter
No
Tangible
Soundtrack
Just
Screens
And
Keypads
Digital
Until
The
Next
Time...

4/29/14

Dangerously

How
Many
Will
Spend
Their
Rent
Money
For show
Money
To
Bey
On
The
Run
While
In
Jays
They
Can't
Afford
To
Throw
Up
A roc
They'll
Never
Get
A
Piece
Of...

4/28/14

The Shoes of School Girls

Imagine
Not knowing
Who
What
When
Where
Why
Or even
How
Or ever...
If
Maybe
Somehow
Some way
Or the
Grueling horror
Of never
Never
Seeing
Feeling
Breathing
Greeting
Being
Them... Again
Imagine
Being them
The 234
The 234
Taken

The 234
Unwillingly
Unyieldingly
Taken
Imagine waking
With dreams of learning
Hopes of becoming more
And your greatness
Your advancement suddenly stolen
And escaping
Isn't an option
Imagine inhaling
The stench of fear
And exhaling hope undetected
The rivers of tears
Streams
That fade
Before
Giving clues
On dry land
Somewhere
In
On
Barren land
Minutes are abducted
In seconds
Innocence is kidnapped
By the truck load
Existence is untraceable
The wailing
The screaming
The threats
Those mothers
Those fathers
Of those daughters
Not knowing

Where
How
Giving your princess
The chance to be better
Could go so tragically wrong
The unknown
The unknown
Imagine waiting until found
Imagine waiting until found important enough to be found
Imagine being
Gone
Until...

4/29/14

Fabric of Our Lives

Bought
Traded
Auctioned off
From
Cotton fields
To
Playing fields
Whipped into shape
From
Royal courts
To basketball courts
Sold to the
Highest bidder
Run
Nigger
Run...

3/17/14

For the Love of God

They're offered bitter fruit
Servicing bored businessmen
And drunken truck drivers
They charge in night
Hoping for Gucci glasses
While defecating on banana leaves
Roadside afternoons
And hotel room dawns
She wants to buy a TV
And shiny utensils...
They pair
And dance in stained sheets
Until her presence is no longer needed
And all that was paid for has been done
And no more
She gawks at flickering lights
From televisions
Dreams of being the first
To bring a radio to her village
Pricing life
To buy one
They traffic
Yellow lines
Dividing pavement
Hard
Rural
Still undergoing development
While battles rage within
Infection claims poverty

And chases promise
Turning children into prostitutes
And parents into pimps
Giving birth to profit
And death to tomorrow
Swallowing fear
And virus
Only to beg for her next meal
She's served the greenest, tartest of limes...

4/21/14

Harvest

Had I known you were
So damn sweet
I would have tasted you sooner
Gone to work for us sooner
Now that I do
Now that I do
Now that I do
I'll take my time
Enjoying the fruits
Of our labor...

4/21/14

Most Importantly

And I want
On average
The next 2,880 Saturday
Mornings
Minus mournings
Just beautiful sunrises
Even when rain surprises
With cleansing downpours
And ending droughts
Lounging tangled limbs...
In linen
Pancakes
With egg whites
And you right
By my side...

4/19/14

Mother's Nature

Wind in that fro
Sun on that skin
Honey molasses
Beams
Stream
From within
Lips on her flesh
Chocolate
Brown
Sugar...
A decadence
That numbs stress
While these
Hands build
From her womb
She gives
Life
And in
Her smile
Is the
Glow
That
Conceives
The joy
Of witnessing
The moon
During the
Heart
Of night...

5/1/14

On the Rocks

Stroking the currents
Of this mighty Mississippi
Taking sips from the mouth
Of mother earth
The oasis of birth
Drunk in love
Drunken love
Liquored
Racing down chin
Limbs...
Limp
Steps stagger
Pulled into subject and matter
Enveloped by honey
And imagination
And the origin of creation
The Overflow
of wine
Communion In the divine
Universe
Comets explode on this
Light force
pour more
Pour more
Sip until full
race down limbs
Lips
Chin
Until heads spin

Spending evenings
in resting fruit
And mornings in
The same
Addictions proven
in nude
Passed out in the flow
overdose
Of crown royal on ice...

5/10/14

Shackle Free

Inspire
In
Me
A
Magnificent
Effort
And
I'll
Do
Anything...
For the
Taste
Of your magic
Even if
Sacrificing my sanity
Inspire
In me
Effort
To neglect
The norm
And mundane
Inspire
My excitement
To
Live outside
Of boxes
And without uniform
And latches
Inspire

In me
Divine
Freedom.

4/14/14

We, Intentionally

Want us
Want you
Want i
In a way
That
Relentlessly
Patiently
Courageously
Speaks
Five different...
Languages
But is
Interpreted
As one
Native
Tongue...
Love
Be my
All encompassing
In a way
That only
Sees yellow
When you cross
My mind
Yet appreciates
The varying shades
Of blue
Assist in
Widening the scope

Of my perspective
Be my authentic
And
We've all been
Humbled
Hurt
And through
Some shit
Be willing
And
Eventually
We'll abandon
Apprehension
And listen
And apply
Want us
Want you
Want i
On purpose...

5/1/14

Gingkaloba

And this time
I don't desire
Praying for amnesia
Or some psychological
Rewiring procedure
No need
To be
Somebody else
No new P.O. box
No relocation
No new name
No previously half told lie reclaimed
No wishing what happens didn't
Or distance
Between memories
Create with me
Reasons to recall everything
This time
No wishing to be anyone
Besides me
Create with me
Reasons to recall everything
Now
Tomorrow
And sixty years
Later
With
No
Regrets

Completely
Thankful
I lived
To experience
We...

4/10/14

Body of Ink

I wear these scars
Better than I could any tattoo
Experience and survival have driven deeper than any needle
Leaving behind impressions that out last ink
Every breath
Symbolic of battle and joy
Ever so often a new one is engraved
A trophy in some instances
Attached to a face, place or name
The others...
Well the others
I anticipate the moment they'll fade...

5/4/14

Red Flags & Hindsight

Every time i clean
I find something
That belonged to you
Reminding me that you were
Here
And we once were
And, although
We seemed to be there
We probably
Should
Not
Have
Ever
Been.

5/10/14

Technical Difficulties

We
Text
Tag
Chat
Instant
Message
Without
Emergency
Or
Rapid response
We
Post
Update
Upload
Archive
Album
Cart
Bond
Over
Likes
And
Shares
Popularity
Over timelines
And stares
No sense
Of urgency
To live
Beyond

Screen names
Alternate
Identities
We friendslist
Keep up
Without
Keeping
In
Touch.

5/11/14

For Those Unworthy of You

Ego will regret not
Having the opportunity
To show
Your past, your best
Your future will
Will thank you
That you didn't...

5/12/14

If They'd Punched A Celebrity

Numbers
Rise
Numbers
Fall
Nonetheless
No less
Be it
196
Or 298
They
Are
Still
Missing
While
Mass media
Outlets
Focus attention
On hands
Being thrown at Hova
By Beyonce's
Little sister
My... God
My little sisters
Our little sisters
Are waiting
Praying
To be rescued
While we
Take selfies
To exhibit

Our idea
Of being selfless
Mimicking celebrities
Whose hashtags
Have made
Our little sisters a trending topic
The value of
A little sister
The value of our little sisters
Outnumbered by juicy gossip
And what's current in the kingdom
Are they not
Worth more than
Sharpies to poster boards
And self-absorbed behavior
Catchy statements and 160 characters
No bodyguards to restrain an army
No Bey to stand at their side
No protection
No assistance
No surveillance
Where's the outpour
The outcry
For their cries
Where's the outrage
30 seconds in an elevator
With 5 people
Who've safely
Returned
Home
Has covered every
Reliable sources homepage
While
They
They
Have no clue if they
Ever will.

5/16/14

Screwed, Wired & Nuts

We
The bolt tighteners
Nut
And screw replacers
We
Who
Rewire
Daily
Battle
Spinning wheels
Jammed bumpers
Honking horns
To beat 8am
Out by 5pm
To sleep
On pillows
Fluffed
Each morning
To live a life
Not seen
In our dreams
We
The play runners
For someone else's
Team
We
Tears
Blood
Sweat

And years
In hopes
Of cashing out
Or in
Before we casket
Rat racers
Spit shining
Spinning rubber and rims
Mouse trapped
By the tails
Chasing cheese
We
The sustained
To maintain
The throttle
Of an engine
Who's full body
We won't embrace
We the muscle
Within the motors
Of them
We feed to endure
We money
We status
We entry to upper level
The constant
Investors
Into someone else's
Vision
We
Hopefully
Soon to be tired
Of being bolts
Screwed
Wired
And nuts.

5/18/14

The Classroom

And then I recall
There were tears shed
The appetites loss
Hurtful realizations
And verbal battles
And confidence shattered
Like glass
And value
Value, felt broken
You felt strange
And ugly
And rotten
Bitter to the taste
And the reasons
Why you were enjoyed
To begin with
Felt distant
And pointless
And I purged
And I released
All that lingered,
Except
The lessons.

5/19/14

Rebirth

And although
I'm still healing
And recovering
And I've even
Endured resuscitation
On several occasions
You love me back to life
Found me
When i was such a mess
A wreck
Out of breath
Whispered out of what
Could've been an early death
Kissed me out of numbness
I've been restored
Taken off life support
Learned to breathe
With ease
You love me
Back to life...

6/6/14

Post-It For the Pessimist

Don't let me
Miss experiencing the warmth
And beauty of the sun
For always
Expecting a slight
Possibility
Of showers
Or chance
Of partial overcast
Please don't
Let me
Miss the sun
And even if showers
Come
Let me
Appreciate the cleansing
Of rain
And know the sun soon show
Just
Let me not live
In expectance of downpour
Or blindness by choice
To the rainbow...

6/4/14

Thank You

They'd ask
Tauntingly
Making my somewhat okay
Horribly noticeable
Playground commentary
During elementary
Middle school jokes
During physical education
And no one could ever
Provide me with exercises
Powerful enough
To strengthen my
endurance to
Work through
This dilemma
Suddenly something
Is wrong with my okay
I recognized the differences
When garments
Were removed
But I
Was okay
I didn't need it
Pointed out
And up for discussion
You don't think this
Young prince
Didn't know
His equipment

Was different
He was built a little different
You didn't think
He
Knew how he looked
Even with unwanted c cups
And monthly visits
By indicators
Of unwanted realities
You don't think he liked
The way he looked
Or did his complex beauty
Baffle you to the point
Of insecurity
Angular facial features
Deepening voice by 12
Awkward
As hell
caught between the middle
Not what you think
And not what anyone could ever figure
This was bigger
Than your average high school drama
Surviving the pointing out
The whispers
How can one be so cool
Yet be treated like winter
She asked
Do you like looking like that
Do you want to look like that
Answer is
So much growing went into
Loving and accepting this vessel
To stop falling asleep
Mid-prayer nightly
Wishing to wake up either just like

You
To make it more comfortable
to exist around folks like you
Or to be fortunate enough
To wake the way I wished
In truth
You
Don't think I know
The way I look
Sick of breaking mirrors
With my fists
Finding beauty
In the beaten reflection
Of my existence
I know
You don't
And that's no longer
My problem.

6/17/14

Masterpiece

Waking at daybreak
To witness the sun's rise
A stretch
A smile
A touch
Room painted in yellow
Mornings colored in awe
Mornings painted in pulchritude
Mornings painted in radiance
Mornings painted in you.

6/4/14

Office Space

Wages fluctuate
Right along with
Tolerance
Respect
And consideration
And folks are tired
And reserves are low
And patience is thin
And folks are tired
Of leaving off latches
Packing lunches
Rising early
And
Returning late
Spending more
Time with strangers
Than themselves
And folks are tired
Of hoping for everything
Working for something
And earnings spent
Wiping away grief
Wages are too low
For no
Respect...

7/24/14

Blessings & Bandages

I never want to
Deny my bruises
My contusions
My wounds with scabs
That vary in size
My layers
My leftover outlines
From bandages
Because
Dammit I survived
And as those wounds
Close and heal
I'm just as grateful
For the experience
As I am for the new skin
I am just as grateful
For the tragedy
As I am for the triumph
I survived
And so did my perspective
Torn
Tattered
Trampled
Renewed.

8/10/14

Untitled

Nooses and night sticks.
Hoods and badges.
Branches and concretes.
Mourning crowds gather.
Watch them sway in the wind.
Our treasured seeds.
Sprout to become gauged fruit.
Southern trees.
Shepard breeds.
Hoses and tasers.
Chokeholds and handcuffs.
Arrested development.
The stench of brutality.
Immune to casualty.
The restrained.
The detained.
Called home.
The morbid refrain.
T-shirts frame.
Hashtags.
The pound.
The splatter.
The nonexistent value
For the fruits of our labor.
The funk of 400 plus years.
Roped. Cuffed.
Murdered.
From leaves to the root.
The corner stores to the stoop.

Rise up Nat
Rise up Harriet
Rise Up Shaka
Pull out our guns
Keep our dollars
Build our schools
Create our banks
Grow our gardens
Kill the dependence
Awaken the resistance
Consistently
Fire our rifles
Impact where it counts
Watch our bullets fly
Watch our bullets fly
Slaughter the beasts
Mangle the pigs
Destroy the systematic genocide
Rise up Huey
Rise up Malcolm
Watch our bullets fly
Consistently
Slaughter the beasts
That haunt our land.
Slaughter the pigs
That steal our youth.
Watch our bullets fly
And pierce the bellies
That ravage strange fruit.

4/16/15

Confession

Let's be honest
I sought you
Because I was taught to
Seventh day of every week was occupied by you
Prayers every night, were audible requests and gratitude to you
    Grace and mercy
Hallelujahs and scriptures
Yet still searching for a connection to you
Tear stained cheeks
Joy filled heart
Happy to have made it through
But the question remains
Was it truly because of you
This packaging you've given me
Has caused more headache and hurt
And to become me
Unraveling so bandages is increasing my work
Load
Psychologically exhausted
Had you no love for
The vessel you created
Delivered yet castrated
Numbers not adding up no matter
The direction in which they're calculated
 Oh I get it
You've put no more on me than I can bare
Right?
My story is a victory I must share
Right?

Who turns men like me
When our souls are in critical care
And we're bedridden from the time we're investing to become this
    proverbial hell
Outsiders merely witnessing the results of T shots, pills popped or
    Androgel
Embracing me as a novelty experiment or in worse cases, a traitor
Yet to you
I'm supposed to remain faithful on knees before altars
The same manipulated entity
Introduced by slave masters
Shackled by regret
Caged by flesh
Panicked and patched up
Mouth worn from begging as a child I'd ask you for nothing more
Than to wake up with a penis and to be her boyfriend
Around 9th grade I became weary
Around 12th I figured you didn't need me at service
Bouncing between Islam, Rastafarianism and Ifa
She became my girlfriend
Perhaps, I owe you residual praise for the latter
I don't hate the Ra I've discovered
But when you built me
Could you have not done your job
Better?

11/17/14

Infinity & Beyond

And you're right...
we never know...
we'll never know until we try.
Until we live this.
Become this.
Endure this.
Be fearless.

12/19/14

In Search of My Sun

And then I realize
Your birthday is Monday
Which explains the low energy
Odd dreams
Ongoing feeling of sadness
And you would've been 9
And so handsome
And intelligent
And probably as tall as me
And breathing becomes shallow
And my chest becomes tight
And the wind becomes so cold
And warmth is a memory
And my heart breaks the same time every year
And I think of you everyday
Wondering what you'd be like
Why you were taken
Why I was chosen
And if you know how empty winter is
Without the beam in your eyes
The glow of your presence
And the radiance of your smile
My sun
My son...

11/24/14

Autopsies of the Living

Sick of shaking heads
Sick of humming spirituals
Sick of dust to dust
Sick of fired artillery
By unfired authority
Sick of earth becoming a compost
For black bodies
Sick of southern, northern, eastern and western trees
Bearing proverbial strange fruit
Sick of the wind
Carrying the stinch of rotting flesh
Sick of thinking that before conversations
About birds and bees
There will be dialogue about surviving
The police
Sick of the spilling of crimson
Sick of murals
And t-shirts
And gritting teeth
And turning cheeks
And protesting briefly
And relinquishing power
Safeties being off
Automatics
Automatically
Sick of being peaceful
Sick of being foot soldiers
Sick of...
Sick of...

Watching
Waiting
Hoping
An oppressive system
Will grant justice
Sick of fighting to live
To be on life support
Sick of hoping
Hands up
Won't leave us all face down
In puddles of defeat
Sick of tears
Screams
And services
Sick of
Sick of
Sick of
Hunting season
Becoming death
By natural causes.

11/24/14

The Stench of History

To think of all the Black bodies
That have laid there
Hung there
Rotted there
In the summer
In the spring
In winter
In autumn
For hours
Four hours
On concrete
On sand
From trees
On roadsides
Drug by trucks
Burned before town citizens
On display
For living
For resting
For breathing
For being
Black
For hours
Bodied
Covered by
The same sheets
As those worn by
Our enemies
On concrete

From trees
Drug by trucks
On roadsides
Burned before citizens
Dead
Like justice
Dead
For hours...

12/28/14

Brown & Garnered

He died with skittles and
Arizona tea in his hands
He laid in the street
For four hours with Nikes on his feet
Accessories made behind bars
Profits gained from our incarceration
And last breath
Visitation
And vigils
Walk to death
Laugh to death
Play to death
Speak to death
Joke to death
work to death
Black to death
breathe to...
can't...

11/19/14

Mother God

There's earth, wind and fire
There's tide and moon
There's time
And only
Because there's you
Sun Goddess
Queen of moons and stars
life protector and giver
provider of essence
and righteousness
and armor
and melanin
and power
and beauty
and love
and authenticity
there's knowledge
and existence
and radiance
and breath in body
And here and now
Because of you.

11/13/14

Becoming He

And for the first time
He's 15
Obsessed with shaving
Revolution
Sports
Automobiles
Science
Lifting weights
And growing up
He's finally growing up
Broadened chest
Lowered voice
Head high
Widened eyes
Bright
And ready for the world
He moves to the rhythms
Of warriors
Raises his dark brown, follicle
covered arms to the sun
Never in his life has he
Felt so alive
So warm
So present
so full of growth
No matter the pain
He's growing
Transitioning
15 and brilliant

15 and becoming
15 and evolving
15 and alive.

11/16/14

Repast for the Living

Sometimes I fear them leaving
As he really starts to show up
Unshaven
Unconcerned
Happy.
Then I remember
They've barely been there
And I,
I denied myself to be present
In the name of what they can handle, love and acceptance
And I thought
How many apologies would be issued
To those witnessing
one dying to live
"I'm so sorry you're going through this..."
Flowers and cards
Lunch dates and "I'm here for you if you need to talk..."
And I worried about losing them
Who never acknowledged me
In full
While one goes through
Forced to fit
Forced to quiet
Forced to turn backs
And I wondered
Why the tears
And farewells
When he shows up
Only wanting to live and be loved

While existing
Given roses
And hugs
And, "I'm here for you if...you need to talk."
While I'm becoming.

11/14/14

Sweat

The aroma of love on our flesh,
the imprint of forever on our hearts.

11/16/14

Growing Pains

They second glance
Say I look familiar
Remembering someone I favor
Search for remnants
Pieces
Have "Oh, yeah!" moments
They
Hold on to what they called me
In private
The name she gave me
They now fumble through it
Respecting my journey
Yet hoping to remind themselves
Hoping to remain close
Hoping to resurrect times of years past
And I introduce them to him
Who's been here all the while.

5/17/15

Baptism

And at that beautiful moment,
when her waters crash.
Submerge me,
this is my only prayer.
Let me be sensible.
Let me be sensible.
And welcome the rush
Of her tides taking me down.

5/6/15

Revelations

What's more divine
Than the vision
Given
In your dreams?

5/1/15

Badges of the Same Name

Oh, you
You've always gathered by the hundreds, thousands
At the town's square
To celebrate our demise
Hunted us down
with your hoods, rifles and hounds
Nooses our around necks
Lynched
Dangling from weeping branches
Prayers whispered in last breaths across dust and clay
Cheers echoing
The stench of burning flesh permeating
Unruly
watching us sway and burn
with smirks and deep grins plastered on your caucasoid faces
The joy in your belly
Of watching us
Sway
and burn
You've always enjoyed watching us sway and burn.

4/28/15

FYI: Business Over Bodies

You know who you are,
My sons and daughters
Will lynch you
Shoot you
Burn you
Sick dogs on you
Teach you self-hate
Torture you
Disenfranchise you
Drop bombs on you
Enslave you
Imprison you
Displace you
Sell you
Trade you
Castrate you
Sterilize you
Give you insignificant access to my environments
but never respect you
Feed you lies
Devalue you
Oppress you
Purge of you
target you
Disease you
Rape you
Experiment on you
Steal organs from you
Use YOUR Babies as alligator bait

Destabilize you
Confuse you
Distract you
Consider you vigilantes and thugs
Sever your spines
Your minds
Your spirits
Your beliefs
Your families
And any attempt flourish, collectively
Take everything of you, away from you
With one tiny request from you
no matter what I do to you
Do not throw bricks at my officers
Or shatter my windows.
Disrespectfully so,
America

4/9/15

Who Tends the Trees

Seeds need water not chalk outlines...
Petals covered in dew, not pellets...
Trees chopped down. Forests not protected...
Chipped trunks tells of old injuries...
Dogs still bark up the bases...
Bombed with tear gas when protesting...
Roots buried. Never allowed to grow...
Lives taken before green leaves brown...
Destroyers paid to prune the branches...
Violently attacking attempts to harvest crops...
Disease and destabilization, land to leaves...
Axes to access. Dehydrating the acres...
Before reaching the sky, dying limbs...
Ever watched them droop when mourning...
Praying the young survive changing seasons...
Uprooting the forage is generationally justified...
Who hears the trees when falling...
Who cares enough to cultivate land...
Who provides safe spaces for the future...
Will violators be charged with murder...
Watching dreams of standing be shattered...

5/10/15

The System Be Like

Shut up. Cuffed up. Shot up.
Your right is to remain silent...

4/11/15

Pronouncing Him

Squeezing through pronouns
Easing through H's
Subtracting
That squiggly
Unnecessary
Alphabet
And R's
After h-e's
And f-e
Before male
Erasing
Not claiming
Explaining
Ignoring
Disconnecting
Dissecting letters
Watching question cover the surprised
And ignorance blanket faces who think they have
A clue
"Why would you want to do that?"
Do what?
Live
Be
Become
Enjoy
Smile
Laugh
Breathe
Squeezing through introductions

Sliding through entrances
As
Him
He
Male
Guy
Brotha'
His
King
Man
Self-made
editor of my existence.

4/8/15

If the River Spoke

And the babies and toddlers of our ancestors
Were once used as alligator bait
Postcards and moldings of those images
Are now considered souvenirs
We've been thrown to the wolves and water for years
The cries of those babies
Haunt the drums of my ears
Remember them.

4/7/15

Rough Rides & Arrested Development

Lists continue growing. Walter…Anthony…Michael
Black breaths shortening. Freddie…Rekia…Eric…Trayvon…
    Emmitt
Sick of hash tagging my slain people.
Overdue outrage. Overdue rebellion. Overdue revolution.
Campaigns and slogans. Please, don't shoot.
Hands up or down. Bullets released.
They're even choking us to death.

8/17/14

Successors

Golden
Radiant
Curved
Alluring
Drawn
To
Magnetic
On canvas
Royal
Goddess
We
create
Heirs
To
our throne...

10/2/14

Sleeveless in the City

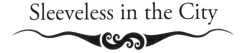

Bullets drive through our neighbor
Hoods disguised as badges
Protect and serve
Crosses that are burned
Bullets know no names
Only melanin
Going against our will
Smith and Wesson
Lessen our presence
No power steering can redirect
The spilling of crimson
On pavement and t shirts
Dampened with wet asphalt
And tears
Hands up in fear
Heads down in reverence
Vigils held in remembrance
Murals cover the cities
Blood spills from the Earth
This Death Isn't color blind
This death is by vicious design
Hard to master peace
While our enemies master pieces
and canines on leashes
The bang and growl
Pop and intimidate
First life lesson
Never crawl
Walk

Wipe
Gurgle
Hold your bottle
Cry
Play
Run
Jump
Laugh
While
Black
From cradle to grave
Engraved
And splattered
This death is by vicious design
Oil on canvas
Red on concrete
Triggers and tanks
Finger paint
Pop and bang
Born to be slain
Laid and beat
Million dollar babies
Tired of celebrating birthdays
Followed by eulogies
This death is their relentless art form
And their armed
Are we?

10/3/14

Web of Destruction

Breaking news
Fear instilled
Control
Directions
Televised lies
Blur our vision
Murders planned
Population decreased
Powers that be enhanced
The decrease
The deplete
Weapons
Execution
Concentration
And FEMA camps
Plastic coffins waiting
Outbreaks
Unleashing
Releasing of viruses
Pay attention
Fed food to dilute our thinking
Slaughtered by artillery of mass distraction
Wonder what's next
Wonder whose neck
Will Be caught on the line
For exposing truth via the net
The age of destruction
Lack of humanity plus corruption
Agendas and plans

The eruption
Of death
And demise
Are you really surprised?
You can't possibly tell me
You've been blinded by headlines
Front page news
They'd never tell us the truth
But Cinemas do
we pay 12.50 to view
what will ultimately
happen to you, you and you
They desensitize
Only to annihilate
Over saturate
Dehumanize in the name of fiction
while releasing clues
We're witnessing implementation
And being toyed with
During our extinction.

10/2/14

Apple Eating Droids

Trendy addictions
Take us petty places
Like hoped for status
To text, talk, web, app
And keep up with the Jones'
We incur travel expenses
Capturing two dollar ceremonies
On devices suggestive of affording destination weddings
We mega pixel
With hard copy faces and books
Relationships
We may never rekindle
We USB and charge
The cost to passport
Attach our net worth
To our image on social networks
We're never idle
Just key board
We
Board
Popularity and never come down
Check-in to checkout
Valued by what we own
Known
For our labels and price tags
Too bad
A vacation doesn't come with airplane mode.

10/16/14

Than the Dark Side of the Moon

You
Glow in the face of night
Sway in the gentle winds
Of morning
Compete with sunrises
Out shining balls of fire
And light
Glistening when touched
Calm when released
Mountains moved
as your waters typhoon
Breaking ground
And barrier
and how beautiful
you are during
Your arrival
And I
at the base of your earth
Rest
Where the lips of shores
Hold tides
and I
Immersed
submerged
as deep as possible
Fall into the crashing
Of the sweetest canal
Body of nectar
and essence of life

Beneath stars
And moon
And sun
And clouds
Leave me
To lay
Surrounded by you.

10/4/14

The Transcending

Every day I erase and discover
Brush away shavings and smears
To uncover
Compress only to unravel
Plant and water
Burying and revealing with the same shovel
Dying to live
The art of transitioning
Embarking on death and life
Now and the after
Ashes and newness
Dust
into the wind
I witness them blend
and scatter
Baptism and eulogy
Communion and committal
In remembrance of me.

10/19/14

Wings

An awkward little boy
Who hated his attire
Hated those ribbons
And bows
And puberty
And shielding himself
Yet finding his place
His reflection
His face
And one day
He studied a caterpillar
Realizing that
One day if God
Granted his wish
He wanted to become a butterfly.

11/2/14

Fire Back

Aren't you tired
Of ashes to ashes
Amen's and ase's
Don't shoot's
And dust to dust
And committals to eternal peace
After eternal war
On life
And bitter
And bullets
And iron in mouths
And on concrete
And wailing mothers
Who kneel over their babies
Wading in puddles
Of DNA and labor
Tear stained hearts and cheeks
Faces printed on t shirts
And hash tagging Black lives
Black matter
Blacks matter
Death becoming trendy
Rage dying as quick as black boys
Black men
Marches
And
tired
worn soles
Aren't you tired

Of being a tired
Worn
Soul
Tired of turning heads
Dodging bullets
Dreams being shattered
Clips
Without cut scenes
Clips unloaded
Bodies bagged
Sidewalks becoming memorials
Walls becoming murals
Memories becoming morgues
Winter becoming death
Summers becoming target practice
And everyday open fire
Chanting down
Calling on ancestors
And Shango
And provision
And strength
Aren't you tired
Of execution becoming routine
And scheduled
And another
and another
and another
And another
Locked
Loaded
Cannon
Boom!

Joshua Kalonji-Alimayu Royster

And every year
At the same time
I recall your conception
The moment my life was completely altered
And every December 22 at 945am
I remember your birth
The hue of your beautiful brown skin
And my nose on your face
Your tiny fingers wrapped around mine
I cried like you when you were hungry
And I cried because I realized
My entire life I had been starving
For salvation
And as you were delivered
So was I
Watching strong little legs kick at the air
Ten cute little toes
Ten little fingers
Eyes that said you were a warrior
More than my son
You were curious
And perfect
And resilient
And fearless
And excited whenever I entered your room
You'd smile and gurgle
I'd marvel at the Creator's miracle
unable to define
Describe

What those moments were like
What they felt like
What holding you felt like
What feeding you
Loving you
Changing your diapers
Watching you sleep felt like
What losing my son felt like
What pain felt like
What breathing felt like
Because since the day you took last breath
The biggest part of me did too.

11/3/14

Like Man, Like Son

I recall standing on tiny foot stools
Pretending to shave my face with them
Growing up
Pulling blades from casings
Placing
Razor sharp to flesh
Mess of madness
Wanting to look like them
Forsakened by creation
Angry with momma nature
Palms covered in anger
Open wounds burning
From shaving cream
And tears and questions
And "Why?" being the word managing
To slip from trembling lips
Having to explain
The abrasions
Cutting away the unwanted
Hoping to make room for the desired
The two of us trapped
One seeking to blossom
The other seeking burial
And we'd stand there
Facing our Reflections
Tracing fear
And hurt
And rage
And a stranger

And a child
A flower choking
Hoping to sprout
Yearning to spring forth
Willing to do anything to blossom.

11/4/14

Missing In Action

He's spent so much time boxed in
That the brown of cardboard is starting to blend in
With his melanin
Changed the packaging
On several occasions to be accepted
Himself and the outside world, he neglected
Claustrophobic
Caged to be displayed
For the liking
Masked to be forever unidentified
No one would know him if he went missing
Not even him
Not even him.

11/11/14

Without Honorable Mention

And we don't discuss her
The Oddball
The awkward
The stepchild
The Unwanted
We remember her occasionally
We acknowledge at times
But silently
Behind shut doors
Tightened jaws
Lowly whispers
And enamel
Her existence scraping the roof
Of mouths
Hollow
Empty
Confidential
Side eyes
Slanted lids
And tears
We dare not mention her in public
For the comfort of those who don't even know
She existed
We
We don't bring her up
We just don't
Only...only him.

11/12/14

Asphalt & Daily Reads

Shots ring more than school bells.
First words. Coached. Basketball. Don't shoot.
Headlines. Chalk outlined. Newspapers and concrete.
Ink leaks. So does blood. Stained.
Marching. Foot soldiers. Worn out soles.
Marked for death. Dying to live.

1/11/15

Love Scars

Sweat in open wounds
Flesh salted as nails dig
Deeper
As I
Deeper ...
We deeper
Tears stain shoulders
And forevers resonate
Promising
Lifetimes
And love
and flesh is torn
and arrivals reached
and the sting
is ultimately ignored
until morning comes
and the sun beams on beautiful brown
and radiant smiles
And my Palm
To your face
tracing soul
And union
while tattooed wounds
Settle
By nightfall
Each of them torn open again.

1/6/15

Lifted

Memories that smear
smirks across your face
and raise an eyebrow
Even when alone
And surrounded by strangers
are the encounters we sometimes bury
Yet hold close
in great detail
Inhaling top lips
And fingertips.

4/25/15

When Morning Comes

We pillow talk fantasies
Waking with wet dreams on lips
hips
Hands
Arms
Chest
Breasts
Backs
Stomachs
Legs
And fingertips.

4/6/15

Beats By

Very little contact,
Rarely, do we dial outside our headphones
And who the hell needs new friends
When I always have my ear buds
Tuning out is so convenient
ignoring is even better
We stay to ourselves
And socialize through limited characters
Most familiar, with our eardrums and thumbs
We live on the run
She said, "I put mine in to look unavailable,
sometimes nothings even on."

4/5/15

Aisle 3

Eventually, I knew, our paths would cross
And I hoped I'd look as dapper as you recall
As effortlessly confident as you were attracted to
With an aura so calm
and relentlessly magnetic
I hoped you'd dig your nails into my back when we embrace
And palm the blades of my shoulders
Greeting me, smile first
Breasts second,
and you did
Leaving the impression of my scent
In your garments and psyche
And I remembered what you smelled like before we touched
I hoped you ached for me when I walked away
I also hoped you'd text or call me
Once we both paced beyond aisle 8
I hoped you'd battle with confessions
still hold our memories sacred
Scroll through our candid captures on Polaroid
And remember just how good you had it
And in the curve of your mouth
I hoped you journeyed into our conversations
And the echo of my name through your lips
That would wake neighbors and raise your diaphragm
and sweat and orgasms passed between the two of us
I know you...the hug says you could never forget me
You could never forget me
And you have yet to
I hate that I still wish you'd show it

Once we part ways
I hate that my hands were shaking
And that I remember how long it's been
and I actually uttered that information audibly
I hate you appeared so excited to see me
Yet you allowed me to leave.

4/3/15

Water Boy

Remember those little boys?
Who dreamt of being football players
And policeman
And strong and tall and grew up
breaking records
And slid through puberty
And acne
And publicly realizing girls were no longer icky
And "going together" with cheerleaders
Was big business
Along with learning to shave
And being a son
A nephew
Chest pumping
Nurtured to become men of the house
Lowered voices
Dominance and authority
Then there was I
Who sat idle with energy that reflected such
Angry with adolescence
Existing openly
Living in private
In dreams
Stealing kisses with cheerleaders
Being someone's boyfriend
Who knew me before I did
Who saw me before I believed evolution to be possible
Me
Romancing anger

Courting despair
Wanting to throw footballs
Wanting to chest pump
Stopped in my tracks
When told
This is
Reserved for boys only
Like jockstraps and beards
and how was I to convince you...that I was...I am
Wishing you could read my soul
And I'd instantly become what I feel
signed...
The boy you wouldn't allow to try out for your squad.

4/2/15

Blood & the River Jordan

And the winds chariot
The stench
Of cargo
Of KJ
Of ancestors
Of Eric
Of last breaths
Of rotting bodies
Of dangling anatomy
from Southern trees
Of babies
Of women
Of men
Foot to head
Elbow to side
Diseased
Feel them
In the breeze
wails and cries
of mourning
of Michael
Of Baby Bu Bu
of doors kicked in
Of sleeping toddlers
Forced to endure reconstruction surgery
after wrongful raids by officers at the wrong address
Of faces displaced
of whips separating flesh
Of screams

of refusal
of heat
of salt
Of racing hearts
witnessing lives taken
inhale
Close eyes
Imagine
the branches
the land
The ship floors
The fields
The sidewalks
where bodies lay
For four hours
For days
The unmarked graves
Bodies branded with an owners last name
and with every purchase, it changed
of burning lives
Of death
Of barely alive
Of prayers to survive
of post-traumatic
of ashes
Limbs snatched
hacked
and
marching feet
Carrying hosed frames
Sicked on by dogs
Batons
Spit
And nooses
laced
knotted

roped
Cocked
And loaded
Stolen and forced
Remember to breathe
in remembrance of those souls
while standing in line for sneakers.

1/30/15

Oblivious

Neurodegeneratives in the clouds, not kites.
Trails are high. Paths are broken.
Awareness depletes on such beautiful days.

4/1/15

Bloom & Rise

Between limb and limb
I find spring mornings
fresh dew soaked petals
Honey for Oshun
Flowers blossoming
Post dawn peaking
And the awakening
Of earth
At the arrival of your sun.

2/7/15

To Smile

There's a gentle pause
And incomparable melody
Heard in the words, "I love you."
That bring music to your life
Giving you a need to dance
In the rain
And appreciate the sun
Just the same
In those 3 words
Are rhythm
And respiration
And reason to.

2/9/15

Darkest of Skies, Empty Arms

And it was on this date
Different year
One morning
The wee hours
You left me
Held you
Wanted to
Trade places
Give my life
So that you could have a chance
I held on
Cradled you
Memorized the shape
And color of your eyes
Held you so close
Watched you look at me
And do the same
Cradled my little warrior
So, so close
Held you close
Bright eyes studying my features
You held on too
As long as you could
Held your little hands
You held my pinky
Took your last breaths
Still looking up
I
still holding on

Held on to you
Held you closely
Talked you to God
And ancestors
Waiting to cradle your spirit
Held you
As you left me
With blankets
That smell like you
memories
Clothing
Furniture
Tears for a lifetime
Bottles
teddy bears
You would no longer hold
felt air
And life
And meaning escape
And tears and unspeakable torture ravage my being
Held you close
Held you
occasionally I feel you near
It was on this day
My sun
Would shine no more
My son would shine no more.

2/17/15

Growing Pains: Becoming He

I reach for razors
And graze the coarseness
of blooming hairs
And memories
That seem so distant
Holding on
Yet releasing
A tiny boy
In bubble gum colors
Rejecting c cups
And lace
Stringing boots
And posing in jerseys
Recalling
Matching ensembles
To theirs
Yet mismatched identities
Binders
Where bras once were
scars where flesh once rose
And curved
Dysphoria and liberation
Not fitting into norms
avoiding circles
Where squares aren't embraced
This
Mirror
Isn't large enough
Wide enough

to reflect
the constant
impact of
Me
Wearing me out
round two of puberty
Delivering me
In a packaging some will never get
Others will resent
and many
May return to sender
reaching
for solace
and the peace of past
While piecing me together
in the present
a gift
I wish would've been wrapped
Differently
contents as desired included
instead of sold separately
have you no warmth
For this young man
Have you no heart for this young brother
In mirrors wiping away follicles
and yesteryear
and who I once was
While unveiling who I've always been
Yet who I'm becoming
I can't ask you to imagine this life
as I have spent far too much time
Placing myself in my own shoes
This
Reflection
Ain't easy
Dying to live

Living to pass
exiting to enter
rinsing away particles
in hopes of becoming whole.

Ships & Sells

From auction blocks to prison yards.
Plantation fields to industrial complexes. Pipeline.
Cheap labor to the highest bidders.
Cotton picking to north face stitching.
Shackled wrists and ankles now minds.

3/31/15

Eulogies in the Wind

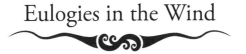

Remember when their ships carried us.
Remember when they broke the levies.
If only these waters could talk.
Unmarked graves, tides, and even trees.
Mother Nature knows us very well.

3/16/15

Living for Self-Approval

Removing unwanted flesh and unacknowledging people.
Binding away chest and negative energy.
Embracing my manhood, losing certain contact.
Becoming me. Butterflies leave cocoons alone.
Boy in the dark, no more.
No sister. No girl. Correcting, necessary.
Bandages and scars. Openness and freedom.
Your brotha'. Your guy. Your warrior.
Transitioning to live authentically without shackles.
Dying to be me in essence.
Becoming is to inadvertently pass. Ase'.
Man of this extraordinary, misunderstood experience.
Choosing to live courageously and honestly.
My comfort is imperative, not yours.

4/19/15

Oil On Canvas

Hands blend
Into skin
Forcing melanin to brush
And stroke
And collage
And canvas
And splash
And drip
Never to dry
From end to end
Corner to corner
Soaking layers
Compressing hues
Splattering
Blanketing
Surfaces
Seeping through sheets until you and morning arrive.

4/16/15

Mirrors & God

There are days
When
Following my shower I sit or stand
Intentionally
Nude
No towel
No distractions
No haste
Just my vessel and I
 Alone yet together
Gazing over
Examining
Crook
Curve
Angle
Placement
Sage burning
Candles flickering
Examining
My spiritual
My presence
I told a friend that I had to make sure
I wasn't so involved
With my ancestors
Spiritual practices
Simply because somewhere beneath the layers
I
Was Angry with
The notion of the God I grew up knowing

And that my pulling away from
Tradition wasn't a matter of my horns showing
This
Body
Bare
Coming with explanation
And questions
And answers
And reassuring myself
That creation makes no mistakes
And becoming is freeing
And these cages
Have suffocated me long enough
Have I ever been angry with my Maker
Have I ever resented You
Questioned You
There's no better sound than silence
And the tears of release
That soothe when trickling
Even though transitioning is passing, evolving and dying
Ashes yet alive
Committal as well as communion
I can say
There
Is no anger
Only awareness
No discontent only discernment
Twiddling thumbs
And guidance
As each eye embraces each pore
Of flesh
In erasing
I've surfaced
Forced to acknowledge
In sight

At times
Painfully honest.

3/26/15

Loving Venus

Every morning
Her clouds
Envelop my rising sun
Every evening
I become her moon
Submerged in her dark matter
As the tides elevate and flow
With every oblige to her wishes
I quilt her cosmos
With my shooting stars.

12/3/14

Unable to Be

Bodies thrown overboard
Bodies hung from trees
Bodies rippled with bullets
Bodies unable to breathe
Bodies packaged like cargo
Bodies festering with disease
Bodies enslaved and imprisoned
Bodies unable to breathe
Bodies stretched across railroad tracks
Bodies unarmed, forced to swallow screams
Bodies massacred
Bodies executed
Bodies targeted
Bodies bleed
Bodies bloody Mother Earth
From sea to shining sea
Bodies taken
Bodies in chokeholds
Be it ropes
Be it police
Black bodies
Blue, purple and blackened Black bodies
Unable to be
Unable to breathe.

4/12/15

The Memory of You

Every time
The clouds crash
And thunder rumbles
My mouth waters
And I recall the way in which her showers
Storm upon me.

4/12/15

50 Years Later

Badges, bullets and chokeholds
Are synonymous with nooses and hoodies
I don't know who's next
I don't know who's neck
Will meet death
In the fold of pale arms
Or who will be silenced
While sirens scream
And phone screens playback
The final breath(s)
As lists lengthen
We're running out of space
And graves
And urns
And tears
And patience
And explanations to our youth
And listening ears
And tactics to survive
And grieving hearts
And BLACK lives.

4/10/15

Outro

Spare me your bravery speeches
Your dropped mandibles
Widened optics
And lumps in throats
Spare me your hugs
When convenient
And your kind sonnets when your schedule allows
The day I loss my first born son
The majority of me passed along with him
So when discouragement quilts me
And loneliness smothers me
And somber, agony
Whispers, come hithers
Of my existence into eternal darkness
it
is
Nothing
New
Yet and still
Where are you?
Those moments when your wrist watches
May not be equipped for spared time
And donated conversations
And charity upliftment and you'd have to volunteer
Where are you?
When the portions of my remaining
 Ponder escaping
This realm
And those too busy to respond

Fail to realize
I just may not, tomorrow
Or the next day
Or the next year
Where are you?
When "this" becomes too deep
And my honesty offends you
Or frightens you
When contemplations
Of morbid, grim
Pontifications
Cloud my sight
With eternal serenity
Where are you?
When I'd rather leave
And lay
Than suffer born
This way
Who will hear me, comfort me
Of despair?

62080766R10080

Made in the USA
Charleston, SC
01 October 2016